# 'Valiant

Discover the Esther in You

---

Jasmine Sepulveda-Molina

# VALIANT

Published in the United States by Enthrall Publishing, Kissimmee, Florida.

VALIANT: DISCOVER THE ESTHER IN YOU
Copyright © 2019 All rights reserved.

This book or parts thereof may not be reproduced in any form, stored in a retrieval system, or transmitted in any form by any means—electronic, mechanical, photocopy, recording, or otherwise—without prior written permission of the publisher, except as provided by the United States of America copyright law. The material contained in this book is provided for informational and encouraging purposes only. It is not intended to diagnose, provide medical advice, or take the place of medical advice and treatment from your personal physician. The author in no way claims to be a medical doctor. Readers are advised to consult qualified health professionals regarding fasting and/or treatment of their specific medical problems. Neither the publisher nor the author is responsible for any possible consequences from any person reading or following the information in this book. If readers are taking prescription medications, they should consult their physicians and not take themselves off medications without the proper supervision of a physician. Anyone attempting to fast should always consult his or her physician prior to beginning any type of fast. Unless otherwise indicated, Scripture quotations are from the Holy Bible, New Living Translation, copyright @1996, 2004, 2007, by Tyndale House Foundation. All rights reserved. Photo credit goes to Candid Artistry Photography. For any ordering information or special discounts for bulk purchases, please contact Ahavah Publishing formally known as "Enthrall Publishing" at www.jasminesepulveda.com or jasmine.sepulveda@me.com
Valiant: Discover the Esther in You
Copyright @ 2019 All rights reserved.
By Ahavah Publishing
Printed in the United States of America

**ISBN 9781082130236**

## Dedication

I dedicate this book to everyone who is seeking the power of a positive mind.

# *In Loving Memory of 5 beautiful souls that crossed over to eternity.*

### Rene Sepulveda
"Grandpa, thank you for marking me with the legacy of Godly fatih. I am a product of your prayers. Love you Abuelo."

### Willie Vega
"Cuzzo, the thoughts of you are forever engraved in my heart. If only we had more time. My heart aches. I love and miss you so much"

### Hilda De Los Santos Vazquez
"Titi, your amazing story of courage, lead me to write and accomplish this book. I want to thank you for always empowering me to be strong at heart.
I love you!"

### Mac aka Macky
"Macky, your memories helped me write this book. Thank you for teaching me to appreciate life, to never complain, and always share acts of kindness to all. Social class and race had no face to the way you honored our friendship. You've helped me understand the true meaning of friendship through Godly love. Your encouragements to follow my dreams have transpired a journey I never thought I could reach. I'm inspired to continue your legacy of "*love without a face*". Macky your rooted in my heart. I love you friend."

### Tiffany M. Long
My dear childhood friend, the week I published this book I learned of your passing. It is all the more reason why this book needed to be published. Thank you for the laughter and memories.

## Thank You

Thank Yahweh above all else for gifting me with the talent to write and empower the world. Also, a special thank you Catherine E. Storing for inspiring me daily to write and publish each book my heart desires. To my beloved husband Jose Molina thank you for always encouraging me to be my best. Areliss, Jeshua, Zion, and Zayn the four of you are one of the core reasons why I enjoy writing. Dad and Mom, I am who I am thanks to the both of you and thank you for never giving up on me. Gerson and Danny I love you! Ms. Josie I am blessed to have you as my mother-in-law, your faith and prayers have helped me soar and go from glory to glory just like God has promised. Natalia Acosta thank you for sharing tears and building me up during the highs and lows. Omar and Sue, you both came into my life during the writing of this book. I want to thank you from the bottom of my heart for all the encouragement during process and completion of this gem. May the Lord bless you both forever.

## Table of Contents

| | |
|---|---|
| Thank You | 4 |
| Disturbance | 8 |
| SECTION I: Disturbance | |
| Esther | 14 |
| Emotions | 27 |
| Procrastination | 38 |
| Anxiety | 50 |
| Depression | 62 |
| Insecurities | 70 |
| SECTION II: Enough is Enough | |
| Happiness | 76 |
| Peace | 81 |
| Faith | 85 |
| Love | 88 |
| Courage | 91 |
| Conclusion | 94 |
| | |
| About the Author | 95 |

## Let's Connect

I have created a FREE gift for you! Visit my website www.jasminesepulveda.com and subscribe to receive a monthly FREE newsletter that will include all the updates that are to come!!! Here are just a few to mention, as I look forward to hearing from each and every one of you!

Enthrall Newsletter includes updates on the following:

- Daily Devotional Registration
- Heart -2-Heart (my personal blogs)
- Webinar dates and times
- Transparency Magazine topics of each month…and so much more!

# More

Want to find out more about Jasmine's up and coming projects and her empowering fundamentals for breakthrough?

**Follow Jasmine Sepulveda-Molina online, by visiting:**

**Website:** www.jasminesepulveda.com

**Facebook:**

www.facebook.com/jasmineauthorselfpublisher/

**Instagram:**

https://www.instagram.com/jsm_ahavah/

**YouTube:**

https://www.youtube.com/channel/UCMGoDT2dYfpyumDiXtJOUmQ?view_as=subscriber

**Email:** jasmine.sepulveda@me.com

## DISTURBANCE

How many times within the first hour of the day do you speak negative about your life or situations? How much time do you spend dwelling on the same negative thoughts? Have these negative thoughts converted into days, months, or years of bitterness and hate? How long will you continue this type these projected thought patterns? Before simply answering each of these questions grab a pen, note-book, and a hot drink and find a comfortable location to relax and evaluate yourself. This book will be a journey of deep cleansing within the soul and mind. Together we will learn to pierce between emotions (spirit) and soul (the real you). It's important to be brave throughout this process, you may want to give up but you can't give in.

The evaluation of self determination is supremely important while navigating through life. Far too often, from generation to generation the passing over of negative habits is taught and lived out as a norm daily. My goal in writing this book is to empower you to know that you do not have to live with the conditioned mindset of self-doubt, pity, unhappiness, instability, jealousy, or even hate.

One of the first steps to understanding the molding process of possibilities is knowing your childhood background. Your thought patterns were learned as a behavior taught and witnessed by your loved ones. Secondly, everything you desire of bringing forth out of life begins in your mind. Thirdly, it is crucial to recognize the stumbling blocks in your life. The stumbling blocks to your pathway of destiny are presented to you by form of habits, behaviors, spoken words, and people. It is important to be very careful who you surround yourself with. Parents should instill within their child early on to be aware of the type of people they should open up to when sharing life events. Not everyone who surrounds you is trustworthy. Some people are for you and others will bash you secretly. When this occurs you may not find it visible at first, it takes time for the real intentions of people to reveal themselves. Sadly, one of the bleeding methods in which people reveal themselves is through jealousy, we will discuss this topic further in this read.

Meanwhile, open up your heart to be honest with yourself. Your mind will process what you hold in your heart. There will be days when you will sense nothing is worth living for or better yet fighting the good faith battle. But know this the mind is the battlefield and you are the warrior on the soil ground ready to combat the snare of the enemy as well as yourself. We our own worst enemies at times and it's time we put a stop to those negative thoughts that surround us daily. The power of the word of God reminds us that we do not need to accept every negative thought that comes to our minds. Our deepest desires and thoughts are known on to God, and He is willing to see us through every moment in life good or evil. But first we need to find ourselves. Cluttering thoughts lead to insecure habits that don't allow us to see the bigger picture. When we are unable to see clearly out minds are fogged eventually blurring out the noise that surrounds us leaving us completely numb to the reality of this beautiful thing called life.

Keep in mind that reading this book may get a bit uncomfortable. In it you will encounter self confrontation. You need to face yourself and be honest with what is really going on within you. Sometimes we think because our thoughts are not spoken aloud, our behavior goes unnoticed. If you have been thinking like this, I will remind you that the thoughts travel to the heart leading to behaviors that become habits, and habits become character.

Therefore, before we begin find reading location that will help you develop a secure mindset to think clearly. Schedule a routine for this read. You may want to have a cold or hot drink on hand to keep you hydrated for the thinking processes as well as a notepad and paper. Write down each and every thought that comes to mind while learning the better side of who you are and why you think the way you do. Before we begin this journey together let's pray.

**Strengthening Prayer:**

Father God in the mighty name of Jesus, I pray for each reader to take this opportunity as a leap of faith to trust you to get to know themselves more than 1 hour ago, yesterday, the day before, or even a year ago. I rebuke all demonic forces that would try to hinder Your divine purpose in the lives of each reader. I cast out every distraction that would try and hinder Your people from reading this book. Jesus, compel each reader to know that You are for them in every area of their lives regardless of what their current circumstance presents before them. There is no greater love than Your love for each and every one of us on the cross. You have died and resurrected for our salvation and deliverance in our minds. Therefore, help us understand that this moment is ordained by You. Thank you Yahweh for what you are doing behind the scenes of each and everyone of our lives. You alone deserve all the glory and honor. Have your way in our lives and teach us the power of Your Word, prayers, fasting, and praise. I pray in advance that the enemy takes his hands off each reader spiritual and mental growth. Your children belong to You alone God. Defend them Yahweh. In the mighty name of Jesus I pray.

~Amen.

VALIANT

## Esther

*For if you remain silent at this time, relief and deliverance for the Jews will arise from another place, but you and your father's family will perish. And who knows but that you have come to your royal position for such a time as this?* ~Esther 4:14

Esther is one of my favorite protagonist in the Bible. Her courage speaks from the heart of God. Her childhood consisted of being a low-income orphan girl who was raised by her cousin Mordecai. When Mordecai adopted Esther they both resided in Susa the metropolis of Persia which is now known as Iran. Susa was an ancient village built from mud stones. We can only imagine Esther's living status as a humble young girl in a simple home with great ethics but no materialist riches. She did not have the influence of a woman figure

14

to guide her steps in simple daily living. She was raised by her single male cousin Mordecai who raised her as his own daughter, one who could not teach her the duties of a wife, but the basics Biblical principles. Mordecai is known for "sitting at the king's gate", prior to developing his foretold name. Imagine Mordecai's frame of thoughts as an employee to the royal palace, in all its splendor I'm sure he longed to be apart of such a blessing. But the story of Mordecai and Esther go far from materialistic standards. Esther became one of the young virgins that would stand before King Xerxes and made queen in place of the exiled queen Vashti. This is speaks so many volumes. How does a small town girl become chosen to stand in a King's palace as a possible candidate to become royal queen? Vashti out of disobedience lost her royal crown to lead her assigned generation. This is an example to encourage believers to obey the commands of the Lord. Having the mindset of Vashti could lead to missing out on the great blessings God has stored up for those who he calls by name. Leaving room for the next to accomplish the mission.

King Xerxes set out all his commissioners to summons young beautiful virgins into the presence of the king, among them was Esther. Esther was a young lady which the Bible describes amazingly *"beautiful"*. I don't just believe Esther was beautiful from the outer appearance but the inner as well. She was humble and compassionate. Besides her outer appearance and behavior, Esther knew the God in which she thrived in faith. Esther **_trusted_** God with all her inner being. Mordecai raised her to have a heart after God and to trust in Him alone.

God has a plan and purpose for each of us. He places mighty people of faith to lift our hands when the going gets tough. As a believer in Christ difficult moments will arise. For Esther the thought of being and amazingly chose queen by King Xerxes opened up a gate of abundance of riches and blessings. However, one of her greatest assets was power. This is why through Esther, we must learn to appreciate the loved ones God has placed in our paths for the strengthening of our mind and spirit. You and I, have a spiritual mentor in the form of Mordecai. Think for a moment, who do you turn to when the going gets tough? Who do you recall from your childhood who kept you believing in the Most High? Who can you turn to now for encouragement? It's supremely important to keep these spiritual mentors in prayer if they have not yet passed on to be with The Lord. Because God chose them to lead you into His greatness for a divine purpose. Maybe it's to introduce salvation onto loved ones, friends, co-workers, or neighbors. Maybe The Lord is calling you to encourage and build up those who need words of encouragement to see another day of life. You must know that you are the miracle blessing to anyone who passes by you.

***Key point: How can you make a difference in your path to empower someone else?***

After King Xerxes chose Esther as his bride, God's plan for the Jews people prevailed. Esther was chosen for such a time as this… *"For if you remain silent at this time, relief and deliverance for the Jews will arise from another place, but you and your father's family will perish. And who knows but that you have come to your royal position for such a time as this?"* (Esther 4:14 NIV). God is an all knowing God. He knew Esther had what it takes to save her Jewish people.

Haman was a high official who served king Xerxes as a government official. Each time he walked in the palace the eunuchs would bow down to honor him with respect. However, Mordecai refused to do so without any remorse. Two government officials Upon Haman discovering Mordecai not bowing down to his presence decided to shift matters for the worst. Haman was a form of Hitler. In 1933, Adolf Hitler was the politician and leader of the Nazi Party. Hitler is responsible for the millions of deaths which took place in the Holocaust as well as the World War II.

Similar to Adolf Hitler, Haman as a high official to King Xerxes, had ultimate power as well. In the book of Esther chapter 3, Haman was given great power and plotted to assassinate all the Jews. Haman also expected Mordecai to bow down to him as a form of reverence to his new found position. Mordecai being faith filled remained faithful to the One true God Yahweh, and refused to bow down to Haman. As Haman grew the seed of pride and hate in his heart, because Mordecai refused to honor him. Mordecai prayed for wisdom. Though Mordecai was being disobedient in the sight of man, to God he remained faithful. Though Haman summoned the threat to murder all the Jews we can only imagine the disencouragement Mordecai must of have felt. As a simple man, according to Esther chapter 4 Mordecai was in such great distress he tore his clothes, mourning, and weeping. Mordecai felt great hurt for the evil that Haman was plotting against his nation. Fearful for the lives of the Jews, who had nothing to do with Mordecai refusing to bow down to Haman, he ran to King Xerxes palace gates. Upon arrival Mordecai was not able to enter the palace, because of his sackcloth. Therefore, at the outer gates he pleaded with the eunuchs and Esther's female attendants to send her the message of Haman's evil plot. Esther wanted clarity on the situation, so she sent for Hathak on of the king's eunuch to get full details from Mordecai at the palace gates. Hathak told Esther about Haman's evil plot of murdering the Jews and how much he was funding the royal treasury for the destruction of the Jews.

## Esther's Wisdom & Emotions

Esther could have ran to the palace gates herself to meet Mordecai in his distress. She too was under great stress, grief, and worry for the lives of the Jews, and Mordecai's broken heart. However, Esther remained her composure. *Psalm 46:10 (NIV) He says, "Be still, and know that I am God; I will be exalted among the nations, I will be exalted in the earth."*

When fear grips the most inner part of your peace, the normal reaction is to expect the worst. Some individuals deal with devastating new with grief or silence. In the desperation of the unknown, the hopes of handling the situation with personal strength almost always seems reasonable. However, trying to figure everything out, without consulting with God leads to deeper brokenness.

Like many of us, Esther received some devastating news. Mordecai the father figure from Esther's youth, was at the palace gates in great distress weeping profusely and unable to meet with her because of his attire. Even in those ancient times the appearance mattered. But this story is not about Mordecai's appearance or getting through the palace gates. It is a profound story that relates to this modern day society. God loves us so much that he sent his only begotten Son Jesus Christ to die on the cross so that we may live*"John 3:16"*. However, Mordecai symbolizes you and I, running and pleading to Jesus for God's approval for our nation's salvation! The sum of our nation is; our family, friends, co-workers, acquaintances, neighbor, students, children, youth, adults, elderly, president, government, and all religious views. This desperate plea to save our nation by the power of God, is not about race, color, or social status. This is about eternity. The time here on earth is borrowed. There is a heaven and there is a hell. The problem is that we don't hear it preached as much as before, because our society is sugar coated with grace. *Woe to those who call evil good and good evil, who put darkness for light and light for darkness, who put bitter for sweet and sweet for bitter.* (Isaiah 5:20 NIV)

We need to stand in the gap for those we know who do not serve or know Jesus Christ as their personal Lord and Savior. Esther was the advocate for the Jews, she had a connection to the King. This is equally similar to Jesus being bridge point for the lost. He is the only one who can connect us to Yahweh, the true living God.

The enemy was operating behind the scenes of Haman's heart. In the same manner Satan will arise and try to challenge your faith. If you refuse to bow down to him, he will threaten your life, the life of your loved ones, and the opposition will begin to oppress you. The way to defeat Satan is through fasting, prayer, and reading the Bible daily. By remaining faithful to The Lord Satan can't entice you to fall into his deceitful traps of death. God reminds us, *"Be strong and of good courage; do not fear nor be afraid of them; for the Lord your God, He is the One who goes with you. He will not leave you nor forsake you."* (Deuteronomy 31:6 NKJV) Do not be afraid of Satan or what he may attempt to threaten you with. GOD IS WITH YOU! How far can

Satan get with your life, if you're surrounded by God? Simply Believe.

Mordecai knew exactly were his victory would come from so he went directly to the source. Though he was pained, crushed in spirit hardly getting words out. He begged for the life of the Jewish people. Esther was chosen as the vessel the would declutter her nation from ruins. Therefore, we too must know where our strength comes from, our Lord our Defender, our Healer. God is the only one who could free each and every one of us including the broken people around us from the dark era of judgement that is going to catch the world by surprise. Nonetheless, the coming of Jesus Christ with our God Yahweh should not take us believers by surprise. The word is a consistent reminder that we are to remain watchful by fasting and praying.

Upon Hathkah's return to Esther, she silenced her fears from all that Mordecai expressed. In return Esther sent him clothing and instructions. *Then Esther sent this reply to Mordecai: "Go, gather together all the Jews who are in Susa, and fast for me. Do not eat or drink for three days, night or day. I and my attendants will fast as you do. When this is done, I will go to the king, even though it is against the law. And if I perish, I perish."* (Esther 4:15-16 NIV)

## Esther's Assignment

By now, we can only imagine Haman preparing his army to destroy and kill the Jews. Setting up blueprints to corner families, children, and hopeless people. But Haman's assignment was going to be canceled first! As mentioned earlier, Esther was an orphan girl. Prior to becoming the Queen of Persia, Esther was limited to the knowledge of royalty. Still she persevered, taking on the opportunity to challenge herself against all the other young bachlorette only to be the one to catch King Xerxes' eye. When God has his eye set on you, know that you are chosen. You can't run. You can't hide. You can't bury your own shame. He already knows and sees your mess. No one but God, can dust you off into your chosen assignment. Stop fighting with your own strength. You're prolonging the process.

God is not going to give you the full picture of what to expect once you begin believing Him for greatness. You must trust the process in order to watch His power unfold in your life. You are already equipped with all the tools needed to fulfill His purpose in your life.

Have you prayed for your Nation fervently? If not I challenge you to close this book for the moment and pray. Pray a prayer that comes from your heart.

**Prayer Thoughts:**

_____

_____

_____

_____

_____

# *Emotions*

### Control the roller coaster within!

*For the word of God is alive and active. Sharper than any double-edged sword, it penetrates even to dividing soul and spirit, joints, and marrow; it judges the thoughts and attitudes of the heart. Nothing in all creation is hidden from God's sight. Everything is uncovered and laid bare before the eyes of Him to whom we MUST give account.* ~Hebrews 4:12-13 (NIV)

Picture yourself in a desert, the landscape is that of hot sand, humidity, low precipitation, dead trees, dry weeds, cactuses, scorpions, and camels are a few of the things that may come to mind. When the mind is full of overwhelming negative thoughts, you may find yourself stuck in the drought of fatigue, without strength for movement. The mind is the most powerful function in the human body. The words out of your mouth have the power to give or take life away. *The tongue has the power of life and death, and those who love it will eat its fruit. ~Proverbs 18:21(NIV)*. Therefore, it is important to know that you have power. The manner in which you influence yourself dictates your future, which includes the type of people and scenarios that surround you short or long term. We are to be very careful as children of God wording our thoughts aloud. Sometime internal meditation is a great method to keep our thoughts under control. But what happens when negativity overpowers positive energy? Negative thoughts become stronger during the cognitive reasoning that there is absolutely no positive change in a person or situation that they may have no control over. Those repetitive thoughts forces the mindset to convert into the deserted battlefield.

A negative mindset is a desert very few thoughts thrive in dry places. Complaining, murmuring, fault finding, hate, rage, anger, angst, anguish, annoyance, anxiety, boredom, depression, despair, disappointment, disgust, distrust, embarrassment, envy, fear, frustration, grief, guilt, horror, hostility, humiliation, jealousy, loneliness, lust, outrage, panic, pity, pride, regret, remorse, resentment, saudade, shame, suffering, wonder, and worry are a few of the emotions that become the scorching sun that dries up all possible forms of life thriving thoughts in the mind. It is easier for people to be upset than be at peace. One possible reason is because the enemy is your opponent and wants to destroy you no matter the outcome. However, God is seeking to war on your behalf and give you a life full of abundance. *John 10:10 (NIV) The thief comes only to steal and kill and destroy; I have come that they may have life, and have it to the full.*

But, the mind is deceitful and so is the heart. *Jeremiah 17:9 (NIV) The heart is deceitful above all things and beyond cure. Who can understand it?* Sometimes we think life will work out according to the desires of our heart and faith, but the outcome of our attitude and actions do not match or add up to what we are believing God to do on our behalf. Regardless, we should be seeking God's will and desire for our lives. When we're in the church we know how to walk the walk and talk the talk. Then at times when we're in our homes or workplace our attitude is reverted to the old ways of our past, because positive change is not happening quick enough. It is time to move past this behavior. Step back and think of the times when your deepest desire during prayer and worship was to do God's will wholeheartedly. There was no need to convince you, because at that moment you knew what God was expecting from you. Now, reflect on the moments when you felt like giving up, you may be experiencing these emotions now. It's quick and easy to lose hope, but living in the regrets of mishaps are the challenge to moving forward. Therefore, brace yourself and stop looking at your current circumstances, look to the future. There is one thing you were created to do and that is to worship

God. He loves you and His deepest desire for your heart, is for you to overcome all negative mindsets and spirits of darkness. Easier said than done but it is true.

One method to managing the mind is morning prayer and devotional. It is an honored privilege to awaken each morning and go before The Lord at the beginning course of each day, giving God praise and glory. The atmosphere sets the tone for the day. Time spent in prayer and devotional, awakens your inner spirit permitting the spiritual warfare to be won in your favor. Without daily prayer the mind wanders, and several moods begin to overpower the attitude and behavior of a person. Prayer eliminates and dissolves this inner manifestation, by bringing peace and confidence through Jesus Christ. Praise and worship, bring an outpouring of The Holy Spirit into your spirit God's glory, In Him you will find strength to overcome negative dry thoughts that urgently need to dwendall instantly. The instantaneous results come when you pray and worship from your heart withholding nothing.

**Revelation 22:1-2 (NIV)**

*"Then he showed me a river of the water of life, clear as crystal, coming from the throne of God and of the Lamb, in the middle of its street on either side of the river was the tree of life, bearing twelve kinds of fruit, yielding its fruit every month; and the leaves of the tree were for the healing of the nations."* In this verse, the from the word of God, John describes that the living water from the throne of God not only gives us life, but also that bears eternal fruit. Though the descriptions of these fruits are not foretold, there is an understanding to the fruit branches from a new tree of life promised by God to those who abide in His truths. As believers should express ourselves with the fruits of the spirit; As children of God the daily goal should be to keep a stead mindset on the Kingdom of God *Matthew 6:33 (NIV) But seek first his kingdom and his righteousness, and all these things will be given to you as well.*

When we set our minds on Christ and the example he left for all believers to follow, there is a consistency in the patterns of behavior on the emotional levels of those who read the Bible, and pray daily.

**Jeremiah 17:9 (NIV)**

*"The human heart is the most deceitful of all things. It is incurable. No one can understand how deceitful it is."* In this passage God is clearly warning all believers to understand that the heart can not be trusted, because our emotions control the mind. The mind is so complex, no one could ever understand the psyche. Psyche is the human mind, soul, or spirit. When God created mankind, the human body was developed from the dust of the earth, secondly God breathed life into the nostrils of Adam depositing within him a spirit and soul *Genesis 2:7 (NIV) Then the Lord God formed a man[a] from the dust of the ground and breathed into his nostrils the breath of life, and the man became a living being.*

Imagine laying before God breathless, without any sign of life and His heart full of love, moves Him to breathe life into your nostrils for, His glory and purpose in your life? Amazing right? Picture yourself in the exact notion. The good news is that He's already done it and if you feel otherwise, He will do it again. Question your spiritual condition. Are you on spiritual life support because of the negative thoughts that have controlled you to the point that your spirit in lifeless? You no longer enjoy what you used to love. Now you need God to breathe life into you like He did for Adam. You want to live again and know that you have a purpose to fulfill, but your thoughts are weak. Remember this, you will conquer and overcome all emotional roller coasters that life throws at you. But first, try to identify what exactly is wearing you down. Could it be a bad habit, sin, toxic people, or are you simply stuck within your own head over thinking everything. Replaying every scenario, how you could of, would of, should of done things differently? Prayer is the filter to unclog the doubts in your mind. It's imperative to trust God with your prayers. Once all your burdens are casted onto Him, remind yourself that you can not take those burdens back. It is pointless to pray with limited faith and than chat with peers about the things that worry you the most. This means you are limiting God to what He can do for you and you do not trust Him. When the mind is overpowered fueled by negative thoughts it's extremely hard to trust God and accept He's working on your behalf.

Regardless of negative thoughts, emotions are the vital way the human mind works. Therefore, to control the emotions from becoming a roller coaster without limits there are 3 steps to consider. *Philippians 4:7 (NIV) And the peace of God, which supasses all comprehension, will guard your hearts and your minds in Christ Jesus.*

## Three Steps to Controlling Your Emotions

1. Identify the Problem find the source - What is triggering the negative emotions?

   _____

   _____

   _____

2. Change your prospective - How can you modify the situation?

   _____

   _____

   _____

3. Refocus, breathe, notice your body language - How can you juggle the three without overwhelming yourself?

   _____

   _____

   _____

Prayer:

*Father God is the Mighty Name of Jesus, we cancel out any demonic force that would intervene with the emotions and thoughts of your people. We pray for peace and clarity in all areas of their lives. Amen.*

# *Procrastination*

*"Get Up and Move"*

Why is that our human minds tend to put off priorities? It's simple, BAD HABITS. Currently, in the generation we are living in the advancement of technology has increased. There are no longer needs to wait in long lines at a grocery store when you can simply log online and place your order and have your items delivered to your door. Think about this you search through your cabinets and refrigerator for some food, though it is full to announce to yourself there is nothing to eat, and decide to place a delivery order. Yes, my friends is the new era we are currently living in at the moment. The new methods of technology clearly project the world at your fingertips. There is no need to run errands like our parents once did centuries ago. At the click of a button what's on the other side of your smart device screen will be at your service within minutes or the span of two days. There are two sides to this privilege. The good and the bad. The good is that you limit wasting time and can focus on what matters to you most, spending time with family, working on projects, or simply relaxing and enjoying the comfort of your own home. Now, all of these pleasurable accommodations come with expensive consequences. The fees for the services are the least of worries. The most a customer is to pay for services is an additional $10-15 dollars. What is harmful about this scenario is the isolation that comes with never leaving your home. You miss out on the beauty of each day, memorable moments with friends and loved ones, including simple exercise.

Procrastination is your enemy, there is no better way to describe it. Procrastination limits the will power of your mind. Lack of discovering your God-given talent. Think back to your childhood when you were full of dreams and aspirations of future possibilities, your imagination was unstoppable. So, what happened? Have you stopped dreaming? Did you lose hope? Or did life just seem to happen and you continued to let it take its toll on your dreams? Some of your challenges with procrastination are rooted from childhood barriers such as family history and ethics. Some cultures learn different priorities with the demand to follow through due to certain beliefs of religion, fate, traditions, and lack of knowledge to know any better from ancestors who failed to teach the next generation.

But you can and will change this awful cycle. Now, you are no longer a child living under the instructions of a parent or guardian. You know this. As a believer in Christ you are to follow the instructions Yahweh *(God "I Am" see Exodus 3:13-15 (NIV) for full explanation to God's real name Yahweh)* has left us his children. The true children of God are peacemakers *(Matthew 5:9 (NIV) Blessed are the peacemakers, for they will be called the children of God).* This

# VALIANT

Biblical truth may be used to make peace with others in all types of relationships. Question, are you at peace with yourself? Do you constantly down yourselves with the TEDIOUS word eventually? Eventually, my life will change...eventually, things will work themselves out in my marriage...eventually, my children will change...eventually, God will show me...eventually, I will begin school again...eventually, I will stop this addiction...eventually, I will stop gossiping. Just STOP! Finding comfort in eventually changing will not happen. It is a false hope of change is lead by the spirit of procrastination. Ponder on this verse *Proverbs 13:4 (NIV) "A sluggard's appetite is never filled, but the desires of the diligent are fully satisfied."* Reread the verse circle sluggard's appetite and underline never filled. This speaks directly to a procrastinator, NEVER will your plans for purpose succeed with the *eventually* mentality. However, the second part of Proverbs 13:4 describes that the *diligent are full satisfied*. It's important to have a motivational mindset and surrounding of inspiration to see results that lead to anticipation. Stop putting things off for later or tomorrow, because you'll never do it. You must condition yourself to live with the now mentality. Now, you have to pray... Now, you have to make the change. .. Now, your life will turn around... Now, your perspective towards your marriage will change... Now, you will speak wisdom into your children... Now, God is showing you... Now, you may begin school again... Now, you will seek help to stop addiction... Now, you will no longer gossip about others. The Biblical instruction to the NOW moment is in **Hebrews 11 (Faith in Action)** *Now faith is confidence in what we hope for and assurance about what we do not see. This is what the ancients were commended for. By faith we understand that the universe was formed at God's command, so that what is seen was not made out of what was visible.*

This profound Biblical truth clearly inspires us to believe in the hope to see life events unfold prior to them even happening. Faith requires moves. You have to walk in the pathway of expectations in prayer. Don't allow your mind to create its own pathway of "what if", declare things as "it is going to happen". "What if" is the pathway to fear. The manner of thinking in fear leads to doubt. How can you possible pray and thank God if you bow down and prayed? You must be careful with your thinking patterns, God is not pleased with double minded thoughts *(James 1:8 (NIV) Such a person in double minded and unstable in all they do)*. James describes in this verse that procrastinators are double minded and they begin one task and jump onto the next project without accomplishing the first. Retrain yourself to think back with the expectations you held as a child. Not that you are going to behave immaturely, but that you are going to dream again with a deep passion of doing the impossible. *Matthew 19:26 (NIV) with man this is impossible but with God all things are possible with God.* Who will you believe, God or yourself? The years have passed you by with no accomplishments of what your heart truly desires. This time around you have to believe in yourself with the guidance of the Holy Spirit? Have you consulted with Him? The Holy Spirit is your "go-to partner" *John 14:26 But the Advocate, the Holy Spirit, whom the Father will send in my name, will teach you all things and will remind you of everything I have said to you.* Be valiant and take your place in the righteousness of God. He is equipping you with the power of the Holy Spirit. If you are alive and well you are not defeated. What is your fear? Why do you live in constant limitation? There is a lot of work ahead of you, but you must put your trust in the Holy Spirit. God promised He will counsel us to the pathways of God's will. Procrastination is a barrier the enemy positions in the pathway of your mind to route thoughts into disbelief about God's power and purpose in your life. The impediment of procrastination has to be broken off of your life and family in the mighty name of Jesus. *Esther 4:14 (NIV) Perhaps you were born for such a time as this.*

**Incompetent: Not having or showing the necessary skills to do something successfully.**

There will be times when you feel insufficient and unworthy. But in these moments trust in God's word. **Nehemiah 8:10 (NIV)** *"For the joy of The Lord is my strength".*
In the moments of weakness God is going to give you strength by the empowerment of your spiritual mentor or loved ones. You must not lose hope in times of despair it will not be easy, but God is trusting you to trust Him. The enemy is the father of all lies. He will try to convince you with that your past mistakes will not allow you to see passed today or tomorrow, and that God never chose you to begin with, however if you're still alive and well God chose YOU! Anything negative you say towards yourself is a form of believing Satan instead of God. Don't fall into his trap, you have great value! You are more than a conqueror… "What, then,

shall we say in response to these things? If God is for us, who can be against us? He who did not spare his own Son, but gave him up for us all—how will he not also, along with him, graciously give us all things? Who will bring any charge against those whom God has chosen? It is God who justifies. Who then is the one who condemns? No one. Christ Jesus who died—more than that, who was raised to life—is at the right hand of God and is also interceding for us. Who shall separate us from the love of Christ? Shall trouble or hardship or persecution or famine or nakedness or danger or sword? As it is written:

"For your sake we face death all day long;

we are considered as sheep to be slaughtered."

No, in all these things we are more than conquerors through him who loved us. For I am convinced that neither death nor life, neither angels nor demons, neither the present nor the future, nor any powers, neither height nor depth, nor anything else in all creation, will be able to separate us from the love of God that is in Christ Jesus our Lord.

Nothing can stop you! You are the only one who can stop your calling. It's time for you to move out of your own way. Procrastination is one of your challenging enemies. The devil will use laziness to prolong your assignment in Christ.

***Equipped: supply with the necessary items for a particular purpose.***

Look within yourself and utilize your talents. What is your greatest passion? What angers you? What makes you happy? Where do you long to succeed? (Take 15 minutes to reflect and journal your thoughts.)

*Romans 11: 29 (NIV)...for God's gifts and his call are irrevocable.*

God is continuously supporting you with great power, only if you allow Him to take control of you agenda. From my personal experience I have found that praying and declaring scripture over your plans, helps guide your outcome. Moments of limitation are over. It's now time to embrace your future and move forward with the enthusiasm you've been missing out on!

### THREE STEPS TO ELIMINATING PROCRASTINATION:

1. What is stealing your prayer and devotional time with God?

_____

_____

_____

2. What is REALLY priority on your agenda?

_____

_____

_____

3. How can you refrain from procrastination?

_____

_____

_____

# Anxiety

*"What are you worried about? Live for today."*

Anxiety is a normal emotion that passes the human mind. Many in this generation speak of anxiety and depression, but do they really understand it? When anxiety becomes a disorder real problems begin to surface. According to the Anxiety and Depression Association of America, Anxiety disorders are the most common mental illness in the U.S., affecting 40 million adults in the United States age 18 and older, or 18.1% of the population every year.

This is crucial to understand. Anxiety has become an epidemic. Now in days, anxiety is influenced by social media, entertainment, and the music industry. Individuals feel as though they have to meet the expectations that the world, when the number one priority in life is to have a strong relationship with God. *Peter 5:6-7 (NIV) "Humble yourselves, therefore, under the mighty hand of God so that at the proper time he may exalt you, casting all your <u>anxieties</u> on him, because he cares for you."*

As you seek Christ in prayer and fasting (refraining from food for a period of time to consecrate with The Lord) you become more sensitive to the voice of God. Learning to discern the voice of God empowers to you shut off the chatterbox in your mind. Anxiety Disorder is the constant method of over thinking thoughts and worrying about the outcomes of scenarios you have no control over. Anxiety Disorder also goes as far as controlling the assumptions you may have over certain people. The way you perceive situations with anxiety intervening can ultimately destroy good relationships. This is the way it is important to establish a relationship with God. Having anxiety is a spiritual attack.

**Spiritual Awareness:**

There are several signs to indicate if you are under the spiritual attack of anxiety. Below are 8 signs to distinguish different forms of anxiety.

1. Know your surroundings: Entering certain locations can grip you with fear for no apparent reason. Before stepping foot in a store, someone's home, or even school/work can cause anxiety. One reason is because the enemy is constantly warring against you so he sets out traps of insecurity and fear to stumble your thoughts. Secondly, during the time spent in certain locations there may be a crowd of individuals naturally doing what they do best...gossiping. Gossiping is a strong tool the enemy uses to distract your perception of others. When confronted with such gossip you can't help to think that if one person is capable of negatively speaking about another. How much more do they speak lies about you? This alone can make a person slip into a panic attack. Insecure people think in this manner nearly all the time, but it's not by default. The enemy is at

work behind the scenes. Thirdly, pay close attention to your breathing patterns throughout the day, heavy breathing, chest pain, and worry can all be aligned with anxiety. Lastly, social anxiety is real, be aware of your body language in large crowds or simply meeting new people. (Consult with your doctor for full details.)

2. Muscle Pain: Body aches and pains may occur for several reasons. One of many is stress. Stress and anxiety can make you tense in the neck and shoulder area ultimately providing a severe headache.

3. Headaches: The tensions of daily life obligations create stressful headaches the intensify with anxiousness of needing to be in full control. The image we women some time portray is that everything needs to be perfect, which is false. Life is not perfect and never will be. However, there are scheduling methods of structure the may give you the pretense of perfection. Loosening up to new ideas and agendas may relieve body aches and headaches.

4. Craving Sugary or Starchy Foods: We all love FOOD! Craving certain foods under stress and

anxiety is common. If things go wrong at school or work, grab a snack, why not? Can't get someone to love you the way you wish, a ½ gallon of Neapolitan ice cream cures a broken heart. All these false pretenses set the mind up to believe that comfort foods is one solution to life's biggest problems. There is a great sensation while eating foods that make you feel great as it slowly makes its way into your digestive system. The issue with this matter is that in the long run serious health problems arrive, such as, obesity, shortness of breath, diabetes, short term memory loss, ulcers, and much more.

5. Digestive Problems: While experiencing anxiety our bodies shift into a "nervous wreck". The fear of things not turning out as expected upsets the stomach with cringing discomfort. During those times a helpful relief will be to take deep breaths and drink water.

6. Moodiness and Irritability: When the mind wonders and is filled with negative emotions, tensions begin to arise. Build up tension causes mood swings and irritability. An awful reality to

this truth is that going through mood swings prohibits the enjoyment of loved ones.
7. Sleeplessness: Consistent worry eliminates restful nights of sleep. When the mind wanders into nightly frustration, the enemy is at work behind the scenes. He attempts to keep the mind entertained with thoughts of *"what ifs"* that will never occur.
8. Lack of Concentration: There could be many factors for lack of concentration. Lack of sleep and bad eating habits are the main ones. A great way to overcome lack of concentration would be to rest as much as possible and drink lots of water. If possible, invest in a life coach who could help you develop a schedule that will suit your daily routine.

The scriptures remind us that we should not be anxious for anything but through prayer and supplication make your request known unto God. *Philippians 4:6-7 (NIV)* *"Be anxious for nothing, but in everything by prayer and supplication, with thanksgiving, let your requests be made known to God; and the peace of God, which surpasses all understanding, will guard your hearts and minds through Christ Jesus."*

Did you know that God cares about your emotions? Did you know that when you hurt, God also hurts. If is weren't so then why would he give His only begotten Son Jesus Christ to die for you on the cross? *John 3:16 (NIV) "For God so loved the world that He gave His only begotten Son, that whoever believes in Him should not perish but have everlasting life."* But as that verse follows through it states that you must believe. When you sit on a chair do you question it to hold you up? Of course not. You "*trust*" and know that the chair was created and designed to hold you up. Then why is it difficult for you to trust The Lord your God who created the heavens and the earth? It's simple, you don't pray prayers of unshakeable faith. It's time to do away with the simple prayers of: "thank you Jesus for this day now bye, I have to run of the fuel of my schedule." No! It's time to create a scheduled time to pray with your creator the

Father who loves you more than anything this world has to offer. Why do you allow anxiety to control you?

***"Anxiety is the soul scrambling for control". ~Beth Moore***

When you lack daily prayers and reading the Bible your soul loses strength. If you miss meals your physical body loses strength you become irritable, weak, annoyed, and at times pained. The same method goes for your soul if you don't feed it spiritual fuel you will spiritually die. You must know who is your source of life! Yahweh, Jesus Christ, and The Holy Spirit. They are the Holy Trinity that hold your world together. Yes, your life is not perfect; many in your family are not yet saved, yes, your not at your fullest potential, yes, you lack finances, yes, people talk about you, yes you are hurt, yes, the pain is real, yes, you feel unheard and misunderstood, but don't lose hope! Jesus already won the victory. *1 Corinthians 15:57 (NKJV) But thanks be to God, who gives us the victory through our Lord Jesus Christ.*

### Fasting and Prayer

Esther knew the power of our God. She understood that without faith in God her people would perish. Her commitment to fasting was first for God and then her people. *Esther 4:16 (NKJV)* **16** *"Go, gather all the Jews who are present in Shushan, and fast for me; neither eat nor drink for three days, night or day. My maids and I will fast likewise. And so I will go to the king, which is against the law; and if I perish, I perish!"* You too need to learn that power of fasting and giving up meals for spiritual maturity and strength in God. You need that type of faith that will remove all barriers of your life. Everything limiting you from conquering your family for Jesus Christ and your own personal empowerment to know God. Fasting is an invitation from above. A special gift to develop strong discernment of the voice of God. The greatest challenge of fasting is giving up food. It is difficult to turn away a warm plate of food for water, fruits, vegetables, or no food at all. But faith produces endurance. *James 1:3 (NIV) "knowing that the testing of your faith produces patience."* Dedicating a set time apart in a season for the sake of spiritual growth will empower you to win over every battle the enemy has presented before you. However, when you fast you break free from anxiety.

    The spirits of darkness are real. Anxiety is a dark spirit. It is one of the highest ranking spirits in the spiritual realm and had been around since the very beginning of Adam and Eve. *Genesis 3:10 (NIV) "So he said, "I heard Your voice in the garden, and I was afraid because I was naked; and I hid myself."* After Adam and Eve ate from the tree of good and evil, immediately the spiritual world opened up to mankind and as you read in *Genesis 3:10* Adam became afraid of God. Anxiety is fear. However, though there are different forms of anxiety know that you have been equipped with the power of God's word to fight the spirit of anxiety. When experiencing anxiety remain calm and think about things you are grateful for in life.

## THE STEPS TO CONTROLLING ANXIETY:

1. Take a deep breath and become aware of your surroundings. Take 5 long deep breaths and remind yourself that this too shall pass.

_____

_____

_____

_____

2. List ten things you are thankful for in life.

_____

_____

_____

3. Consider aromatherapy: candles, essential oils, showering, and relaxing. If possible try and go for a walk.

_____

_____

_____

# Depression

*"Stop hanging your head down low."*

Depression. Do you relate to this ten letter word? Ten dreadful thoughts come to my mind like; sadness, loneliness, stress, worry, insecurity, incompetent, quarrelsome, frustration, jealous, and doubt. This ten letter word list is actually some compared to all the negative thoughts that come to mind regarding depression. But, how exactly would an individual cope with such misery? Depression is the dark place of hopelessness. Feeling hopeless is a deceitful tactic of the enemy to make one believe God does not care about you and it not attentive to your prayers. But I am here to tell you that there is hope in Christ Jesus. He desires to help you in all the areas of your life, but are you praying with expectancy? Are you praying at all? *John 16:24 (NIV) "Until now you have not asked for anything in my name. Ask and you will receive, and your joy will be complete."* It's time for you to ask for God to move on your behalf according to His will for your life. If depression has ever become a part of your life, it's because somewhere along the line you have stopped praying.

Mordecai felt a season of depression in the book of Esther. *Esther 4:1 (NIV) "When Mordecai learned of all that had been done, he tore his clothes, put on sackcloth and ashes, and went out into the city, wailing loudly and bitterly."*
Mordecai felt desperate, sad, fearful, and guilty. The enemy as the accuser made him feel at fault for Haman's decision to murder the Jewish nation, because Mordecai did not bow down to him. Imagine yourself working with a superior who consistently talked down to you and expects you to bow down at their presence. I know exactly what you're thinking (absolutely not!). Those same were the same words and feelings Mordecai experienced as he knew better than to bow down to any other god but Yahweh. But what happens when you sense loneliness for the cause of doing what is right. The enemy will make you feel so awful and accuse you for all the wrong doing on in your life.

Depression is a silent killer. Most people who suffer from depression don't express any type of signs. They go about their daily lives and accomplish most required task with a smile on their face. This explains why most people are shocked to hear of sudden suicides without any prior acknowledgement. Depression begins as a form of oppression. Oppression is the mild stage of depression. To be oppressed is to feel mistreated with control. It's similar to overwhelming stress that makes you feel as if your pinned to the wall. This is a strategic plan of the enemy to make you feel like no one understands your situation. His schemes are to distract you from reaching a complete intimate relationship with God. Satan whispers that God is not listening to your prayers, no one loves you, you'll never amount to anything. Lies! The devil is a liar. After hearing those lies for so long you begin to believe them if you lack in prayer. Prayer is essential to overcoming oppression which then leads to depression. If the enemy could trick you into believing that you are not worthy of being happy then you my friend are not trusting God. You may question how can I trust a God that I pray to and does not answer my prayers? You need to learn how to fervently pray. Prayer has different levels. You can not expect God to change your circumstance with the type of prayer to you pray over dinner. You must pray a fervent prayer that comes from the innermost part of your being. In *Luke 22:44,* Jesus' sweat drops were _like_ that of blood. Jesus prayed fervently asking the Father for His will to be done. In the same demeanor we too should pray with every thing we have within. When you don't know what to pray allow the ask the Holy Spirit to lead your prayer.

Suffering from depression includes the setback from enjoying life, but remember the voice of the Lord today. *John 16:33 (NIV) "I have told you these things, so that in me you may have peace. In this world you will have trouble. But take heart! I have overcome the world."* God is reminding you today that there is hope for you. You have the power to dominate depression. Cancel out with faith any circumstances or medical reviews that label you as depressed. Shake yourself NOW in the mighty name of Jesus and be empowered to start fresh, right in the middle of the hurt you are emotionally experiencing.

### King David

King David experienced a period of depression during his time of reign over Israel. David failed God many times over the course of his life, but God never stopped loving him. David commited adultry, and murder. His actions lead him to consequences of great sorrow and depression. David was troubled and battled deep despair. In many of the Psalms, David wrote of his anguish, loneliness, fear of the enemy, his heart-cry over sins, and the guilt he struggled with because of evil sin. We also see his huge grief in the loss of his son in 2 Samuel 12:15-23 and 18:33. David's honesty with his own weaknesses gives hope to those who are struggling. The same goes for you. Regardless of what you are going through take time to read the book of Psalms. David's spoke his sorrows into prayers onto God for forgiveness, healing, help, and thankfulness in advance though he did not see instant results. David never ceased to worship, praise, and give God the honor He alone deserves. King David's repentance moved the heart of God and with great power, God kept David in perfect peace with the royal promise of agape love and reign over Israel.

    You too are apart of the agape love and royal lineage of Jesus Christ. Shake yourself from everything that has tried endless to limit the great work that God has begun in you. *Philippians 1:6 (NIV)"being confident of this, that he who began a good work in you will carry it on to completion until the day of Christ Jesus."* The simple fact that you are alive today is a vast reason for you to jump for joy and give God glory! That dream inside of you is your calling! You did not place that vision within yourself. God put it there for His glory to be magnified by your praise for the blessing. All you have to do is trust Him *(Proverbs 3:5-6)*, through the process. You are not to stress out and try to figure out the entire outcome all by yourself. It's going to take prayer, consecration, and a team of individuals who love God to help you build the vision. When you don't understand the core principle of *"putting God 1st and trusting Him"* frustration and depression will rule over you. Don't give depression a foothold over your mind. Depression invites itself into your life in the most silent moments of life. While attempting to rest, depression unwelcomingly, shows up in your thoughts. The whirlwind of thoughts repeat themselves over and over again. You try to control the negative talk within, but then you're convinced "it actually makes sense." The devil is a liar! Never give in to the thoughts the enemy places in your mind. Control the thoughts in your head. You have the power to accept or reject them. King David while feeling depressed questioned his soul not God. *Psalm 42:11 (NIV) Why, my soul, are you downcast? Why so disturbed within me Put your hope in God, for I will yet praise him, my Savior and my God.*

## Moment of Reflection:
- What do you do when you pray and pray and see no change?
- Who and what do you put your trust in?
- Are you magnifying God or your problems?

God placed in my heart to end this chapter in prayer. Because the spirit of depression has been upon humanity for far too long. You will come out of this dark season in the mighty name of Jesus.

*Prayer: Father God, I plead with you, to give your servants the hope and joy their heart's desire. God forgive them for past mistakes. Help them know that you are not mad at them. Give them the wisdom to discern your voice for specific instructions. Remove all hopelessness and replace it with joy. Give them new blessings to look forward to each day. In the mighty name of Jesus we pray. Amen.*

*Biblical verses to reflect on:*
*Isaiah 43:1-13, Psalms 118:24, Jeremiah 29:11*

## METHODS TO OVERPOWER DEPRESSION:

1. Slow down. Take time to breathe and realize you're worth. You're important to those around you, and remember "you do matter".

_____
_____
_____

2. Fast. Jot down the reasons why you feel depressed. Pray and fast for your mind be released from all negative thoughts in the mighty name of Jesus.

_____
_____
_____

3. Pray and learn scriptures. Speak them aloud daily.

_____
_____
_____

# Insecurities

*"Know your worth!"*

According to the Bible, there are several figures who have struggled with insecurity. Though they had great faith in the Lord, they too struggled with their own thoughts. Sounds familiar? Let's dive right into this major problem which leads to destruction. As mentioned in the previous chapter King David struggled with depression but was delivered through worship unto God. King Saul who reigned prior to King David also had a deep struggle with insecurities.

King Saul was a great man of valor but lacked self-confidence. He was extremely insecure of David taking his place. Have you ever felt a lack of security, because someone out shined you? Insecurity is a very common issue, because many individuals don't know their identity in Christ Jesus. The book of Samuel reveals several times when Saul doubted himself and God. Yet, with all of Saul's insecurities God still chose Saul to be the first king of Israel. Saul was intimidated by David because he was a mighty warrior in the battlefield. But even greater, David carried the anointing of God which lead David to great endeavors. Prior to David becoming the king after Saul's reign, he was a soldier and best friend to Jonathan Saul's son. In order to keep a close eye on David, Saul observed closely David and Jonathan's friendship. But even before all the jealous was revealed in Saul, when Samuel anointed Saul to be the first king of Israel, Saul was afraid of failing the nation prior to leadership.

Leadership can be a very trying position, but when God chooses and appointes you to lead, there is no room for doubt or fear. God is the master of all designs. If you feel in your heart to lead in any area of your life, chances are that strong desire is exactly where God wants you to be. But being insecure will lead you to make some mundane decisions. You have to take heart, know your place in the hands of God. Knowing your place is acknowledging your skills. Think about those who depend on you to make a difference in their lives. You may not think much of yourself at times, but the reality of life is that you truly matter. Every single pathway of life has a purpose. Whether it's to serve you or someone else. God predestined this very moment. Are you living it completely fulfilled?

King Saul's insecurities lead him to live in a silent rage of hate towards David. God is an all knowing god. He knew that Saul's days were numbered and coming to a quick halt. In the battlefield King Saul and Jonathan died at war. Theologians believe that King Saul took his own life. King Saul lived is such fear of David outshining him that he longed for death.

Insecurity is a silent killer. It's like a fungus that starts off small and spreads like wildfire. The more an individual becomes insecure the less happier they become. Bitterness takes root in their heart, developing an anchor of hate towards themselves and other people.

But life does not have to be full of negative energy. Insecurity and jealousy are certainly not from God. The 10th commandment God gave Moses for the Israelites, was "You shall not covet". When God gave this command he literally meant to banish all envy from your heart. You're not to desire what does not belong to you. For an example, your neighbor's assets, someone's spouse, or long to be like someone else. Jealousy is envy. Take into account this Biblical passage: **Proverbs 14:30 (NIV)**

*A heart at peace gives life to the body,*
*but envy rots the bones.*

Jealousy leads to envy that "rots the bones"! Do you understand how powerful this Biblical principle is to all believers in Christ. We are to remain focused on the Father Yahweh "The I AM". He alone can fulfill the desires of our hearts. When you pray with intentional prayers that flow from your heart with repentance, all things change. You will no longer desire to covet and wish you had what you actually don't need. All you need is to be more like Christ Jesus.

### CONSIDER THESE QUESTIONS TO MOVE FORWARD FROM INSECURITY:

What comes to you easy without much effort?

_____

_____

_____

Where are you needed the most by others?

_____

_____

_____

What upsets you?

_____

Where would you like to see change happen?

Is there jealousy and envy in your heart?

### *Reflection:*

To find the answers to all the thoughtful questions in your mind, cast your cares on the Father. Be honest with God and yourself. Unfilter all your insecurities, doubts, and jealousy. After you are honest about intentional change, make time to be with people who have been forgotten. The less fortunate may need a meal. Someone lying in a hospital may need you to declare the power of the cross over their life. Elderly individuals in a nursing home may also need some company. A loved one may need a phone call from you. When you take time to devote yourself to others, there won't be room for insecurities, because you have discovered the Esther in you is the identity of Christ.

# Enough is Enough! Get Positive

Wow, you have made it to the second portion of Valiant. Congratulations! This part of the Valiant will reflect on positive emotions. The key to understanding how positive emotions work, is to create your own happiness. Therefore, chapters 5-10, are brief, because you are going to write your own positive story. I will simply guide you on how to get started. So what are you waiting for? Let's get to it!

> When writing the story of your life, don't let anyone else hold the pen.

# Happiness

/ ˈhapēnəs /

*noun*

*noun: happiness; plural noun: happinesses*
*the state of being happy.*
*"she struggled to find happiness in her life"*

In this generation the perception of happiness is clearly on social media posts. Everyone has a picture perfect home, cars, marriage, family, meals, careers, and self-image. The truth is that happiness is more than an image. Most individuals attempt to find happiness in the image of someone else. Social media is a platform to be aware of that increases depression instead of happiness. The comparison game is real. It all starts with; "I wish I looked like that, had that, got that, live that, or had been there." The wishing is endless. Why, because everyone wants happiness and acceptance. Rejection is certainly not a good feeling, neither is being marginalized. Have you ever experienced such pain, but then found acceptance and love like never before? If you have yet to find happiness now is the chance to look further than what you have limited yourself to see. Creating happiness doesn't have to be difficult. Think about all the reasons why you should be happy and list them. Then list all the reasons why you are not happy. But first realize that no one but God can make you happy. You can not expect to be happy through your spouse if your married, children, or family. They may each bring you happiness. But they certainly are not responsible for your happiness. Therefore, never put that pressure on them. It's never okay to make your loved ones feel like they have to walk on eggshells because you're upset. Furthermore, create your potential happy list while you are you are in a relaxed positive mood. Think clearly. Go for a walk, shower, and drink water. Refocusing your mind requires intentional effort. You will not get positive results if you try to understand happiness while you're upset. Remember you are now discovering the

Esther in you! Let's pray: *"Holy Spirit in the mighty name of Jesus, look at the heart of each individual commencing to write their story of happiness. Lead them into the path of merciful peace. For some people this is impossible but for you God, nothing is impossible Matthew 19:26 (NIV). Give them strength to be patient during the season of the unknown, which will soon shed light into each reason. Empower the hearts of your people God. We were all created for such a time as this Esther 4:14 (NIV).*

Now that time has come for you to begin writing your story of happiness. Believe me I could have wrote this chapter for you and the rest to come, but true healing comes from within during time spent alone with God. Take that pen or pencil and jot down all that you feel inside. Be transparent as possible. Allow the Holy Spirit to minister unto you. This writing session requires total surrender to The Lord, quietness, and full sincerity that you do want change to happen. Write away beloved.

VALIANT

Date:_____ Time:_____

# VALIANT

# *Peace*

*/pēs/*
*Learn to pronounce*

*noun*

*freedom from disturbance; tranquility.*
*"Jesus said to the woman, "Your faith has saved you; go in peace"*
*~Luke 7:50*

After a regular routined day, the best feeling in the world is listening to the rain from your comfy bed. Bedtime is usually the time when most people find it easy to rest. However, for others it's extremely difficult. Jesus reminds us in *Luke 7:50* that faith produces peace. You must have faith in God in order to receive total peace. You have the power within you to trust God and develop peace. Learn to stabilize your emotions. Talk to yourself with positive thoughts and internal meditation on The Lord. Extensive thought process burdens the mind. Taking time to relax prior to bedtime is the perfect way to get a good night's rest. It's impossible to go into a deep sleep with thoughts of stress in the mind. The first step to relaxing is bathing, then applying anointed oil with essential scents. Dimming the lights and turn on some ocean/white noise sounds. YouTube is a great platform to find nature sounds. Take 5 deep breaths and allow your entire body's weight to sink into your bed. Imagine the ocean and a gentle breeze. Try to relax. Also, think of how important soothing calmness is for an infant to get a nap or a goodnight sleep. You too my friend need nourishment prior to your bedtime. Always take time to care for yourself. You are worth every moment. I encourage you to write this portion the next morning, after a goodnight sleep.

VALIANT

Date:_____  Time:_____

# VALIANT

# *Faith*

*/fāTH/*

noun

*"Complete trust or confidence in someone or something."*

I enjoy taking road trips. Long drives seem to give me clarity on my next writing idea. I begin to visualize the context and inspirational topics. Looking far behind into the rear view mirror, I can't help but notice just how small my surroundings begin to shrink. The outlook ahead of me is much larger. The view ahead is the reality of where I am headed towards. I'm not quite there yet, but I know I am getting closer. Envisioning my writings during driving builds up my faith. *Hebrews 11:1 (NIV) "Now faith is being sure of what we hope for and certain of what we do not see."* Take this time to see what is not completed in your life as if it were 100% done. Writing this portion of your story will create a level of happiness you haven't experienced in a very long time. Without faith it is impossible to please God. Therefore, exercise your faith with full trust in God.

VALIANT

Date:_____  Time:_____

# *Love*

/ləv/

Learn to pronounce

noun

*"An intense feeling of deep affection."*

Love is a passionate word that everyone in the world wants to experience. Love is not a feeling. Love is an emotion given to us, by the Spirit of God, so that we may have grace for others around us. Love requires action. In 1 Corinthians 13, the scriptures detail the true meaning of love. You can gain all that you wish, but if you don't have love you have nothing. Where are you expressing your love habits? Is it only for your family? Are you passionate about serving in the church? Do you serve the homeless, by volunteering your personal time? Do you consider the visions of hope God has planted inside of your heart? Are you willing to take a leap of faith, and move in love to help meet the needs of others. Do you know that desire within to do something is God's vision for you? Write your love story.

VALIANT

Date:_____  Time:_____

# VALIANT

# Courage

/ ˈkərij /
*noun*

*"The ability to do something that frightens one."*

When faced with trying times of decision making, the norm is to panic. Fear grips an intense feeling that the situation magnifies the impossible. Taking courage requires reflection. Take a moment to think about the possible outcomes. Esther did not jump into conclusions, when faced with the news of her entire race being murdered. Esther's emotions could have raged into anger or sadness. But instead, Esther took a stance for her Jewish race and with Godly confidence, declared her nation to fast and pray in the presence of the Lord. You must realize that you need help and that you cannot go it alone. Recognize that God is all powerful, that He has promised to never leave you nor forsake you (*Hebrews 13:5 NIV*). Go to Him in prayer and fasting to seek His will in making the right decision. Then confidently make your decision, with the courage and conviction that God is on your side.

VALIANT

Date:_____  Time:_____

VALIANT

# Conclusion

Life comes with all sorts of challenges, surprises, and ultimately discoveries. Life can be adventurous or dreadful. After learning the tools in gathered in Valiant you should be able to shift life's unexpected turn arounds to the most memorable legacy ever lived.

God is the giver of life. He created you with divine purpose. You are not here as a roaming soul trying to fit in. You were placed on earth to live your life loud for Jesus. Now, that you have written your personal positive story, it's time you live it. Break old habits and develop new ones. If you need further encouragement stay connected to this God sent ministry.

## About the Author

Jasmine Sepulveda-Molina is an inspiring author, editor, self-publisher, founder of Ahavah, motivational speaker, personal life coach, and entrepreneur. In 2010, Jasmine accepted her calling as a minister of God to provide Biblical studies and encouragement for teenagers and young adults. In dedication to her calling, Jasmine also founded Undefeated Outreach Ministry, formerly known as Battered but not Defeated (BBND), located in the heart of Kissimmee, Florida. Undefeated Outreach Ministry, provides meals, clothing, and useful resource to families and children facing hardship throughout central Florida. When Jasmine is not writing or editing, she spends time in the Word of God and Prophetic intercession by healing, helping others to break through strongholds, and restoring family relationships and marriages.

Jasmine also enjoys spending quality time with her husband, four children, and both of her beloved parents. Her passion is reading, writing, and empowering all the nations of the world in these last days, to equip themselves to seek God first, and embrace their ordained assignment since Yahweh predestined their life before the foundations of the entire earth.

Jasmine is a firm believer that every hurdle she has overcome was for each reader who takes the time to read her story.

# Let's Connect

<u>Visit My Website</u>

I have created a **FREE** gift for you! Visit my website www.jasminesepulveda.com and subscribe to receive a monthly **FREE** newsletter that will include all the updates that are to come!!! Here are just a few to mention, as I look forward to hearing from each and every one of you!

Ahavah Newsletter includes updates on the following:

- Daily Devotional Registration
- Heart -2-Heart (my personal blogs)
- Webinar dates and times
- Transparency Magazine topics of each month
- …and so much more!

**Follow Jasmine Sepulveda-Molina online, by visiting:**

**Website:** www.jasminesepulveda.com

**Facebook:**

www.facebook.com/jasmineauthorselfpublisher/

**Instagram:**

https://www.instagram.com/jsm_ahavah/

**YouTube:**

https://www.youtube.com/channel/UCMGoDT2dYfpyumDiXtJOUmQ?view_as=subscriber

**Email:**

jasmine.sepulveda@me.com

SHARE SHARE SHARE…. LET'S CONNECT! THERE'S SO MUCH MORE FOR YOU TO DISCOVER!

"Empowering a Better You"

-Jasmine Sepulveda-Molina

Dear Reader,

Thank you for taking the time to purchase my book and reading it. Your feedback is very important to me. I'd like to ask for a small favor. Would you be so kind to an **HONEST** on Amazon?

Thank you so much!

Be Empowered,
Jasmine Sepulveda-Molina

Made in the USA
Lexington, KY
05 December 2019